T0380966

Love Sees No Color

JER

ILLUSTRATED BY : Ashlynn Simpson

Print information available on the last page

Rev. date: 05/30/2019

To order additional copies of this book, contact:
Xlibris
1-888-795-4274
www.Xlibris.com
Orders@Xlibris.com

"Wake up! Uncle is coming so get dressed," Reece looked at his sister and goes back to sleep.

"Leave me alone Lizzie, I want to sleep," but Lizzie keeps shaking the bed.

"No, we have to be ready," she whispers to her brother.

"Ready? For what? School is out so leave me alone," he mumbles into the pillow.

"Uncle David is coming to get us," Lizzie's face lights up with the brightest smile.

"Yeah, we're going to have fun," Reece springs out of bed and starts getting dressed.

"Mom just doesn't let us go with people like that, Uncle must be special," Lizzie said.

"Yeah, he must have a super power," Reece exclaimed.

"He's here, he's here!" Lizzie said looking through the window.

Both kids ran downstairs, "Mom, Dad can we go with Uncle?"

"Yes, you can leave with your Uncle. Do you remember our conversation?"

"Yes mom, listen to Uncle because he is in charge," they both replied together.

"Can we go? Can we go!" they asked excitedly, "Yes, you can go." Once their mother said those words they raced outside.

"Uncle, what kind of car is this?" Lizzie asked curiously.

"We haven't seen a car like this before!" Reece is excited, he has only seen cars like that in television shows.

"It's just a car, get in now and let's go!" Uncle is so excited seeing them and is ready to hit the road and have fun.

"Uncle I like this car it's pretty." Lizzie says.

"Uncle your car is fast like the race cars." Reece expresses.

"Uncle people are looking at you and your car," both say. "Uncle we think they like your pretty hair."

"No, they are looking at how beautiful you both look," he said "Thank you Uncle, so are you," both children reply smiling.

"This was so much fun uncle."

"Reece lets play a game!" Lizzie and Reece start playing a game to pass time.

"There's corn, farm houses, and out houses. There's your house Reece," Lizzie said.

"There's your house Lizzie," Reece replied.

"Uncle where're we going next?" Lizzie asks.

"I have to feed you right?"

"I'm hungry too Uncle," Reece quickly replies and Uncle says "I'm hungry too." with a smile on his face.

"Here we are, let's go in and eat some breakfast," Uncle says as they pull up to their first stop.

"Here's the menu order whatever you want to eat," both Lizzie and Reece say" Yes, Uncle."

Reece sits next to Uncle with his menu since he needed some help.

Lizzie, is a smart one and smiles because she loves words and needs no help. She's trying to decide what to eat for breakfast.

"Lizzie do you need help reading the menu?" Uncle asks.

"No Uncle, I know how remember?" Lizzie says as she smiles and swings her feet back and forth in the chair.

They place their orders are and eat a tasty breakfast.

"What's next?", Reece said full of energy.

"Lets see what's in the shop next door, they might have something you like?" Uncle took Lizzie and Reece to the Souvenir Shop.

"Uncle I like this truck!" she said, "I will get you the truck Lizzie."

"I like this car because it looks like yours," Reece said, "I will get you the car Reece," Uncle said.

"If you don't see anything else, lets go." Uncle said since they had other things to do today.

"Uncle, there are a lot of corn fields here, it's making me sleepy." Reece said.

"Why is there so much corn? and why are there horse' pulling the carts? We don't see that in our city?" Lizzie asked.

"Well Lizzie, you're in Amish Country." Uncle smiled

"So, Uncle what was the place we just left and the food we just ate?" Lizzie asked

"We left a Bed and Breakfast and the food that they were serving was Amish." Uncle explained.

"Uncle the people were nice and the food was good." Lizzie said.

"Wake up, were here! If you want to swim, go inside the house, change out of your clothes, and put on your bathing suits."

After Lizzie and Reece hurriedly worked together, they excitedly walk towards their Uncle to say, "We're ready, can we get in the pool now?"

He smiles and say, "Yes, but put on some sun-screen, and no running. There's ice cream, water, and candy bars in your room when you want them. I put them there in the refrigerator."

While standing there Lizzie says, "Uncle, I think those people are looking at you."

"No, Lizzie the they're looking at how beautiful and mannered you both are."

"Now, you two go and enjoy yourselves before your parents come to pick you up." He loved Lizzie and Reece as they were his own.

"Lizzie, Reece it's lunch time, come get something to eat" both dashed out of the pool and went to the house for lunch.

Reece and Liz couldn't believe it was lunch time already, "Uncle, it's lunch time?"

One hour of pool and rest later, Lizzie and Reece returned to the water to have fun until their Uncle called them out the pool.

Lizzie ask, "Uncle, can we have a few move minutes?

Uncle replies, "No, your parents are here to pick you up."

Lizzie says "Yes, Uncle."

Lizzie asked, "Mom, Dad can we stay the night with Uncle?"

Mom says, "The next time, you can't change people's plans at the last minute. What do you say?"

Both Lizzie and Reece said, "Thank you Uncle for having us, we LOVE YOU."

Unscramble Words

_____   rac

_____   rcat

_____   norc

_____   oncr efdil

_____   rhate

_____   rehos

_____   olop

Car

Cart

Corn

Corn Field

Heart

Horse

Pool

 Ashlynn Simpson was born and raised in Tampa, Florida. She is currently an undergraduate at the University of South Florida seeking her bachelor's degree in Cellular and Molecular Biology. When she is not working to pay her bills or studying for school, you can find her relaxing by the beach or drawing. At the age of 19, she illustrated her very first published book titled "I'm Not Scared", written by JER, and continues to do more work with the author - This was just the beginning of an amazing friendship.

Thanks to my Loving God Father/Uncle David. A man I have Loving memories of and who taught me that love SEE NO SHADES. My childhood memories of you bring me joy. I miss you although I have not seen you in years. I dedicate this book to you and the time you were there. The times you showed us nothing but love. When you picked up my brother and I in your Corvette and drove us from Jersey to Pennsylvania in your fast car and showed us nothing but LOVE! Uncle sent us home with a bag of 3 Musketeers, Souvenirs, and memories of love that has no boundaries!

Printed in the United States
By Bookmasters